BEARCUB BIOS

KETANJI BROWN JACKSON

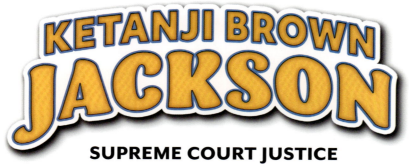

SUPREME COURT JUSTICE

by Rachel Rose

Consultant: Beth Gambro
Reading Specialist, Yorkville, Illinois

BEARPORT PUBLISHING

Minneapolis, Minnesota

Teaching Tips

BEFORE READING

- Look at the cover of the book. Discuss the picture and the title.
- Ask readers to brainstorm a list of what they already know about Ketanji Brown Jackson. What can they expect to see in this book?
- Go on a picture walk, looking through the pictures to discuss vocabulary and make predictions about the text.

DURING READING

- Read for purpose. Encourage readers to look for key pieces of information they can expect to see in biographies.
- Ask readers to look for the details of the book. What happened to Ketanji Brown Jackson at different times of her life?
- If readers encounter an unknown word, ask them to look at the sounds in the word. Then, ask them to look at the rest of the page. Are there any clues to help them understand?

AFTER READING

- Encourage readers to pick a buddy and reread the book together.
- Ask readers to name three things Ketanji Brown Jackson has done throughout her life. Go back and find the pages that tell about these things.
- Ask readers to write or draw something they learned about Ketanji Brown Jackson.

Credits:
Cover and Title page, © H2rty/Wikipedia, © JasonDoiy/iStock; 3, © REUTERS/Alamy; 5, © H2rty/Wikipedia; 7, © ASSOCIATED PRESS/AP Images; 9, © ULora/iStock; 10,11, © ASSOCIATED PRESS/AP Images; 13, © American Photo Archive /Alamy; 14, © H2rty/Wikipedia, © JasonDoiy/iStock; 17, © Fishman64 /shutterstock; 18, © LUNAMARINA/iStock; 21, © Sipa USA/Alamy; 22, © Xinhua/Alamy; 23, © kate_sept2004/iStock; 23, © Alina555/iStock; 23, © Image Source/iStock; 23, © FG Trade/iStock; 23, © IPGGutenbergUKLtd/iStock; 23, © monkeybusinessimages/iStock.

Library of Congress Cataloging-in-Publication Data is available at www.loc.gov or upon request from the publisher.

ISBN: 979-8-88509-801-4 (hardcover)
ISBN: 979-8-88509-802-1 (paperback)
ISBN: 979-8-88509-803-8 (ebook)

Copyright © 2023 Bearport Publishing Company. All rights reserved. No part of this publication may be reproduced in whole or in part, stored in any retrieval system, or transmitted in any form or by any means, electronic, mechanical, photocopying, recording, or otherwise, without written permission from the publisher.

For more information, write to Bearport Publishing, 5357 Penn Avenue South, Minneapolis, MN 55419.

Contents

Top Judge 4
Ketanji's Life 6

Did You Know? 22
Glossary 23
Index 24
Read More 24
Learn More Online 24
About the Author 24

Top Judge

Ketanji Brown Jackson had a big smile.

She was very happy.

Ketanji was the new top **judge**.

Ketanji's Life

Ketanji was born in Washington, D.C.

Her parents were teachers.

They showed Ketanji it is important to help others.

When she was four, her family moved to Miami, Florida.

Her father went to school there.

He became a **lawyer**.

Ketanji was **proud** of him.

Miami, Florida

Ketanji wanted to be like her dad.

She became a lawyer when she grew up.

Then, she worked for a judge.

In 2005, she started work as a **public defender**.

Ketanji helped people who were in trouble with the law.

Her job was to make sure they were treated fairly.

After that, Ketanji became a judge.

She heard about problems.

Then, she thought about laws.

Ketanji said what was right.

In 2019, there was a big problem.

Immigrants were told to leave the United States.

Ketanji said these people had **rights**.

They needed a chance to stay.

Then, something big happened.

In 2022, Ketanji was picked for the Supreme Court.

She was the first Black woman to be a judge there!

Ketanji has helped people her whole life.

And she is not done.

As a top judge, Ketanji will keep helping people.

Did You Know?

Born: September 14, 1970

Family: Ellery (mother), Johnny (father), Ketajh (brother)

When she was a kid: Ketanji colored with her father as he studied to be a lawyer. That is when she fell in love with law.

Special fact: Her name means lovely one.

Ketanji says: "I love this country and the rights that make us free."

Life Connections

Ketanji cares that all people are treated fairly. What do you think it means to be fair? How have you helped make sure everybody is treated fairly?

Glossary

immigrants people who come to live in another country

judge a person who decides the answer to law problems

lawyer a person who helps people with law problems

proud very happy because of something someone has done

public defender a lawyer who helps someone who cannot pay

rights basic things that everyone should have or be able to do

Index

immigrants 16
judge 4, 11, 15, 19–20
law 12, 15, 22
lawyer 8, 11, 22
Miami, Florida 8–9
public defender 12
Supreme Court 19
Washington, D.C. 6

Read More

Rose, Rachel. *Ruth Bader Ginsburg: Supreme Court Justice (Bearcub Bios).* Minneapolis: Bearport Publishing, 2021.

Schuh, Mari. *The Supreme Court (Our Government).* Minneapolis: Bellwether Media, 2021.

Learn More Online

1. Go to **www.factsurfer.com** or scan the QR code below.
2. Enter "**Ketanji Brown Jackson**" into the search box.
3. Click on the cover of this book to see a list of websites.

About the Author

Rachel Rose lives in San Francisco. She grew up in Ireland, where her father was a lawyer. He loved the law, just like Ketanji does.

24